First Published in 2020 by Echo Books

Echo Books is an imprint of Jenkins Family Nominees Pty Ltd, ABN 14 640 032 604

Registered Office: 5/5 Markeri Street, Mermaid Beach QLD 4218

www.echobooks.com.au

Creator: Jeff Hatwell and Elspeth Langford, Authors.

Catherine Gordon, original artwork.

Title: The Swans of Ypres: De Zwanen van Ieper

ISBN: 978-0-6488545-9-3 (hardcover)

A catalogue record for this book is available from the National Library of Australia

Book layout and design by Peter Gamble, Canberra.
Set in Garamond Premier Pro Light Display, 12/17 and Edwardian Script.

www.echobooks.com.au

By the same authors:

Jeff Hatwell: *No Ordinary Determination*, Fremantle Press, 2005 and 2014 and *Brave Days*, Echo Books 2020.

Elspeth Langford: *Miss D: One year in the latter life of a rescue dog*, Vivid Publishing, 2020

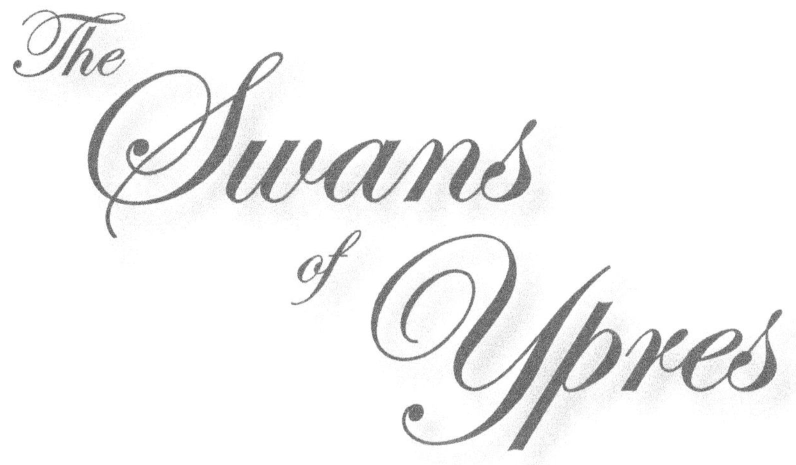

De Zwanen van Ieper

Jeff Hatwell and Elspeth Langford

Paintings by Catherine Gordon

ECHO BOOKS

The City and the Swans

More than a hundred years ago, two European white swans found themselves trying to survive the perils of the First World War. The city where they had made their home was devastated, with its beautiful medieval buildings smashed into piles of rubble. The citizens left for safer places and only soldiers remained, defending the ruins against the invading armies—and the swans stayed too, sharing the dangers faced by the soldiers of the British Empire through four long years of fighting.

This happened in the region of Europe called Flanders, at a small city that had seen many wars and many marching soldiers during the centuries of its existence. The city is named Ieper nowadays, but at the time of this story it was known as Ypres (Ypres looks like you would say it 'Wipers', but the right way is '*Eep*-rr'). The countryside around the city was mostly flat, with many little villages nearby and some low hills curling around to the east and south. The people of Ypres had always tried to live peaceful lives, but it was not easy to do that when kings and generals were often fighting wars over the country around it. All the same, the people worked hard, mostly in the business of weaving and selling cloth, and the city became wealthy over the years.

Ypres in the year 1649: a map and a panoramic view drawn by Joan Blaeu.

There were many beautiful buildings in Ypres, especially its Cathedral and its Cloth Hall, where merchants got together to buy and sell the fine fabrics.

With all the wars going on, walls were built around the city to protect it from armies trying to capture it—huge thick walls of bricks and stone, called 'ramparts' by soldiers. Then they dug a wide ditch outside the walls and flooded it with water from the river that ran past the city, making a moat for extra protection. The roads in and out of the town ran through gates in the wall and across bridges over the moat. On the south was the road to the city of Lille, going through the Lille Gate, and on the east was the Menin Gate, where the road to Menin went through.

In 1830 the city became part of a new country called Belgium. In the following years it seemed that the country, and Ypres, was at last going to be left in peace by its warlike neighbours. The town and its people settled into a quieter existence. The old walls—the ramparts—were no longer needed for protection, so parts of them were knocked down and some of the moat was filled in. Along the tops of the ramparts that were left, on the south and east sides of the city, the citizens planted trees and made walking paths. There they could relax and enjoy a pleasant stroll after work, or perhaps a picnic when the weather was fine. A part of the moat remained as well, a long stretch of water on both sides of the Lille Gate to the south of the city and around past the Menin Gate on the east.

The calm water of the Ypres moat became home to many wild creatures—frogs, fish and especially water-birds. The plants growing in and around the moat gave the birds plenty to eat, and there were reeds and rushes on the banks where they could make comfortable nests. The birds must have thought that it was rather nice of the humans to make this great place just for them to live in! There were ducks and moorhens swimming about, but by far the biggest and most beautiful birds in the moat were the swans. They were the type, or species, called Mute Swans—that doesn't mean that they can't make a sound, just that they are much quieter than other types of swans. They grunt, snort and hiss, not very elegant sounds for such beautiful birds! Their feathers were pure white, their beaks orange and black, and their necks long and elegantly curved. There were not many of them there, because swans like to have a lot of room, but they made an impressive sight as they glided gracefully on the water—although sometimes they looked a bit odd when they ducked their heads under water to get food and left their tails up in the air.

This is the story of two particular swans, a male and a female, who lived in the Ypres moat during the most dramatic time in the city's history. They had not always lived at Ypres. They had been born in different places, with different parents. As is the way of swans, when they were about six or seven months old they had been pushed out by their parents and sent to make their own way in the world. For the next stage of their lives, they both joined a colony of other young swans in another Belgian waterway. It was here that the two first met, during one summer. It was in the year that the humans called 1912, but of course that was neither here nor there to the swans, who only cared about what season it happened to be. Some of the young swans were starting to notice that boys and girls are different. Male swans are called cobs and females are pens, and one of the young cobs (let's say his name was Dirk) found himself becoming very interested in one special pen floating near the riverbank.

He had seen her before, but had not taken much notice of her. Now he suddenly realised that she was really quite beautiful (to people, one swan looks much the same as another, but the swans themselves can certainly tell each other apart!). The young pen—we'll call her Sofia —could see that Dirk was studying her very closely indeed. She was quite happy about that, because she was thinking that he was rather good-looking too. Dirk was a confident young cob, and after a while he decided to go over to her and introduce himself. There was a breeze blowing in the right direction, so he opened out his wings a little and let the wind push him across the water, rather like a sailing boat. Dirk had learned that trick when he was very young; he was now quite good at it and liked to show off!

Dirk gave the swan greeting sign, a quick nod of his head.

'Hello,' he said, in the language of the swans, 'You're Sofia, aren't you?'

'Yes, that's right,' she said, returning the nod, 'and who might you be?' although she knew perfectly well who he was.

'I'm Dirk,' he replied, 'and I was wondering if you would like to feed with me.'

For quite a while, Sofia said nothing and just looked at Dirk, until he began to feel rather less confident than before. Finally she said,

'All right, why not?' and the two began to feed on the succulent plants at the bottom of the river. They ducked their heads under the water, stretching their long necks to reach the plants with their beaks, and waggling their bottoms and tail feathers in the air.

Finding a Home

Over the next two years, Sofia and Dirk got to know each other very well, and the more time they spent together the closer the bond between them became—if they were people we might have said they were engaged. Their personalities were different but fitted together well—Sofia was rather serious-minded and practical, while Dirk was more relaxed and laid-back but he could be determined when he needed to be. Now their instincts told them that it was time to set out together and find a new place where they could settle down as a couple, and perhaps start their own family at the right time. They began flying about looking for the right place.

On one of these flights, they saw below them a beautiful stretch of calm water running around a big group of buildings and a thick wall of brick and stone. It was the moat at Ypres. Dirk was interested straight away, and he called across to Sofia,

'Look down there Sofia, let's try that place!'

'Well, I see lots of silly quacking ducks,' said Sofia, 'but apart from that, it could be all right. Let's go and have a closer look and paddle around for a while.' (Sofia was a bit of a snob where their cousins the ducks

were concerned, and didn't like them very much. If she had known the story of the 'Ugly Duckling' she would have liked them even less!).

Dirk said, 'What about that spot over there?'

It was a stretch of moat with the wall on one side, a wide grassy bank on the other, and a small island in the middle, near a bridge and a gate in the wall—the Lille Gate. There seemed to be an area with no other birds around. The two swans glided down, settled onto the surface of the water, and paddled over to the bank. Sofia didn't take long to make up her mind.

'Yes, Dirk,' she said, 'This will do very nicely.'

There were a few other swans living along the moat towards the Menin Gate, youngsters who would be moving on sooner or later. Sofia and Dirk were the only paired couple there and they had the Lille Gate end pretty much to themselves. There were not even many ducks near that part, which was a good thing as far as Sofia was concerned. If they felt like a change of scene they could always paddle along to the Menin Gate and back. There was usually something interesting going on to see—people in colourful clothes walking around with their children, dogs and sometimes horses. The people often gazed at the two beautiful swans out on the moat—perhaps not knowing that Sofia and Dirk, who both had more than their share of curiosity, were looking back at them with just as much interest.

One day, they made their way to the far side of the bridge at the Menin Gate. There Sofia looked a bit suspiciously at the two stone lions alongside the gate, until she worked out that the strange creatures were just statues and weren't going to come to life. She and Dirk then paddled up close to the bridge for a look at the people wandering past. The other swans in the moat never came this close to people, so Dirk and Sofia soon attracted attention.

They were noticed by two young children, an eight year old girl named Bep and her brother Stefan who was ten. Their parents ran a small shoemaking shop in their house, just down the road from the Gate. Both children loved animals, and they were fascinated to see the two swans floating so close. 'We should try feeding them,' said Stefan. 'Quick, Bep, run home and see if Mama has anything they could eat.'

Bep dashed home, grabbed some vegetable scraps from the supper their mother was making and ran back to the bridge. Stefan was waiting impatiently and the swans were no longer in sight.

'What happened to them? Where are they?' Bep asked anxiously.

'Don't panic, they're just swimming back down the moat. Come on, we'll catch them up.'

The children crossed the bridge and walked south along the bank. They soon spotted the swans drifting lazily on the water. Bep went right to the water's edge and called out:

'Here swans! Here swans!'

'Not so loud, you'll scare them,' said Stefan, but the swans were gliding towards the bank to see what all the noise was about.

When they were close, Bep tossed the scraps onto the water surface. The swans poked the food around for a while, then decided it was all right and ate it up. Just a small snack for them, but the children were delighted.

The swans went on their way again, heading slowly back in the direction of the Lille Gate. The children followed them along the bank. Finally it was getting dark and time for Bep and Stefan to go home.

'They must live down that way somewhere—that would be why we haven't seen them before,' said Stefan.

Actually, Dirk and Sofia hadn't finally decided to stay at Ypres, but the two friendly young humans helped them to make up their minds. After a few weeks living in the moat, they came to the decision that this was the place to spend the rest of their lives together. Everything seemed peaceful and safe, there was plenty to eat, and the children came down to the water to visit whenever they could, usually bringing some treats with them. The swans could not have known that things were about to change completely.

The Coming of the War

This was the time that humans knew as August 1914 and after nearly a hundred years of peace Belgium suddenly found itself involved in another war. This time it would be the worst war that the world had ever known. A huge army from Germany invaded Belgium, with the idea of marching through it to attack their main enemy, France. Belgium had no quarrel with anyone but when foreign soldiers invaded their country they fought back with their small army. Soon Britain joined in too, helping both France and Belgium to fight the invaders.

At first, the armies bypassed Ypres, then one day in October Dirk and Sofia were sailing along the moat, sightseeing and having something to eat, when they noticed something very unusual happening on the land. A long column of men on horses appeared, trotting up the road and clattering across the bridge into the town. They were all dressed the same, and on their heads were odd-looking sharp-edged helmets. There were rifles slung on their backs and they held long spears in their hands. Altogether they looked rather fierce.

'What's all this about, Dirk?' asked Sofia.

'I don't know, but I don't think it's good,' was his reply.

Albert I, King of the Belgians

Nothing much seemed to happen, however, and the next day the horsemen rode out again and went back the way they had come.

What the swans had seen was the first time—and as it turned out the only time—that German soldiers got into Ypres. They were only a group of cavalry scouts, but the main German army was not far away to the east and north of Ypres and heading towards it. If the Germans could capture Ypres and then march to the sea, they had a good chance of winning the war. But now there was another army approaching, from the other direction. It was the British, and their soldiers were on the way to stop the Germans from getting to Ypres. Meanwhile French soldiers, and the Belgian Army with their brave young King Albert, blocked the way to the sea.

A week after the German horsemen had come and gone, Sofia and Dirk saw some different soldiers tramping towards the town from the west. They went into the town and after a while came out again at the other side, through the Menin Gate and across the bridge, and then marched out of sight towards the hills to the east. These were the British, in their greenish-brown uniforms and round flat caps, all carrying rifles. For the next few days the swans could hear a strange crackling sound coming from the east, as well as many louder thumping noises. Clouds of smoke started to appear on the horizon.

'I've never heard anything like that before,' said Dirk, 'I wonder what it could be.'

'Lots of new things are happening these days,' was Sofia's comment. 'We knew this was going to be an interesting place to live, but I didn't think it would be *this* interesting!'

Over the next week or two the noises grew louder as they came nearer. The distant crackling became the constant loud bangs of rifles shooting, and the thumping became the roar of artillery shells exploding out towards the hills, some in the air and others making huge holes in the ground. Often Sofia and Dirk would see wounded soldiers coming back across the bridges into the town, with bloodstained bandages around their arms, legs or heads, limping or carried on stretchers by other soldiers. There were many more lying out in the countryside who would never come back, but they had stopped the German army, and a time came when the noise of the rifles did not come any closer.

But there were other ways to fight the war. One day in November Sofia and Dirk were resting on the outer bank of the moat when they heard a new sound, a whistling and whizzing in the air, coming towards the town and rising to a scream as it got closer. They could see the tower of the Cloth Hall rising above the ramparts, and as the scream stopped there was a deafening crash, a flash of flame and a cloud of black smoke on the tower wall. Pieces of stone crashed down into the street. As the smoke blew away the swans saw that a large hole had appeared in the tower. They were not close enough to be hurt, but they had felt the shock wave in the air.

The terrified birds scuttled to the water and began paddling back towards the bridge. Sofia was the first to calm down a little, and she stopped to look back at the scene. Dirk stopped too, feeling his heart beating very fast.

'Well, whatever next?' said Sofia, rather shakily.

'Here comes your answer, I think,' replied Dirk, as they heard the whizzing sound again, followed by the crash of the explosion. This time the flash was out of sight behind the rampart, but another puff of smoke shot up and broken bricks flew into the air. They were artillery shells that the Germans had started firing at the town itself, instead of the fields in the distance. More and more shells screamed down. Roofs and walls crumbled and fires broke out in some of the buildings. A cloud of smoke formed over the town. One of the shells missed the buildings and hit the top of the rampart, knocking away pieces of brick that splashed into the moat.

'Come on, let's get back to our spot,' said Dirk, 'This is getting dangerous,' and they swam back to the Lille Gate bridge as fast as they could go. Here they were further away from where most of the shells were falling, and Sofia had the idea of getting under the small alcoves of the bridge for protection. The water level was high and it was a bit of a tight squeeze, but the solid stone above made them feel safer.

After a long while, the shells stopped falling. Now the townspeople could be heard calling out to each other in fright and anger, together with the firm voices of soldiers giving orders. Sofia and Dirk cautiously poked their heads out from under the bridge.

'It seems to have stopped now,' said Dirk, 'but I have a feeling those things will be back soon. Maybe this isn't such a good place to live after all.'

'We'll have to leave here before long anyway, you know,' replied Sofia.

'Why is that?'

'Haven't you noticed the weather is getting rather cold?'

'Oh yes, you're right, it will be freeze-time soon,' agreed Dirk. 'If we need to go then, it won't be too far though. There should be a few places near here where we can find something to eat.'

Swans are not particularly bothered by cold; their feathers keep them fairly warm in winter. The main problem is finding enough food if their home water freezes over and they can't get to the plants on the bottom—big birds like swans need a lot of food. If that happens, they move for a while to somewhere with plants they can reach to eat; they can even eat grass if they have to. It wasn't long before Dirk and Sofia noticed that the moat was beginning to freeze up around the edges, so they took off and flew west towards the coast. They had not gone very far when they found a field with an irrigation ditch, and enough plants and grass to eat and patches of bush for shelter. It was a good enough spot to spend a few months until the weather started to warm up again.

Dirk had been right about the shells—they came again and again as the German guns pounded the city all through November. The citizens took shelter in the cellars underground as many of the houses crumbled under the explosions of the shells. Like everyone else, Bep, Stefan and their parents spent most days cooped up in their cellar while the shells crashed down outside. One nearby explosion knocked down a wall of their house, so even when they could come up to ground level, the freezing weather got in. The British soldiers in the town went into the cellars for protection too, and they used the ramparts for shelter as well. The brick walls and roofs of the ramparts were so thick that the shells could not blast through them, even though they sometimes knocked pieces off the outside. There were old rooms and tunnels dug under the ramparts and the soldiers used them to make safe offices, resting places and hospitals. The bombardment slowed down later in the winter and things had become a little quieter for the people in Ypres into the new year of 1915. It was still dangerous though, and many of the buildings had been destroyed. For Sofia and Dirk away in their winter spot, it was time to make a big decision.

Whizz-Bangs and Babies

Signs of warmer weather meant that Sofia and Dirk had to decide whether they should go back to their place in the Ypres moat, or look for somewhere a bit quieter and safer instead. The swans soon agreed to give the moat another try—it was the first home that they had chosen together, and their instincts told them to return. Before long, they were winging their way east again, and the town was coming into sight. Things had changed in Ypres while Sofia and Dirk had been away. As they glided over, they could see that the moat and the ramparts looked much the same, although the trees on the ramparts seemed very ragged, more so than just from losing their leaves over winter—but in the town itself many of the buildings were wrecked, and those that were still standing had big holes in the roofs. For a moment, the swans thought the shooting had now stopped, but then there were three or four flashes on the far side of the city, and they heard the crack of the shell-bursts and felt the bump in the air. The war was still going on.

There were piles of rubble in the streets and hardly any people were moving around; most of those were soldiers, all looking the same in their uniforms and carrying rifles. The fields outside the city were marked with craters torn out by explosions, and there were long lines of trenches with more soldiers crouched in them, keeping below ground level; in some places where water was too close to the surface for digging, the soldiers had piled up walls of sandbags instead.

'What a mess,' said Dirk, 'do you still think we should stay?'

'There's our spot down there,' Sofia said cautiously, 'it still seems to be all right. Let's go down and take a closer look.'

They swooped down to the water. Their place in the grasses looked just as they had left it, with none of the big holes that had been blasted around the city. For now, it seemed that the exploding shells were not coming near that area. They could not see over the city walls from there, so that hid the wrecked buildings and made them feel a bit better.

'Let's give it a try, for a while anyway,' said Sofia, 'it's still a good place. Besides, did you notice that none of the other birds are around? We can have it to ourselves—without any ducks!'

'You and the ducks! I think it's more important that there don't seem to be any other swans anywhere now. More food for us. All right, we'll stay, for now at least,' was Dirk's reply. 'I hope it works out, because I'm getting the feeling that it will soon be time we had our own babies.'

The artillery shells still crashed into the town often, but the swans began to get used to them as a part of life nowadays. They did not have a word for shells, so they thought of them by the noise they made—'whizz-bangs.' As it happened, that was the word the British soldiers used for one kind of artillery gun. Their settling spot stayed fairly safe, and with their keen ears the swans were getting better at hearing the whizz-bangs coming from a long way off. They could usually paddle to the Lille Gate bridge before most of the shells hit. If they were too far away, they could at least go to the foot of the rampart for protection. Of course the British soldiers had plenty of artillery guns too, some of them positioned quite close to the city. Sofia and Dirk soon worked out that these were shooting their whizz-bangs in the other direction and so were not dangerous. They did make a terrible noise when they fired, though.

When they had been back a few weeks, the feeling came over Sofia and Dirk that it was time to do their first mating dance on the water—that might be the swan version of getting married. They circled about, copying each other's movements, dipping their heads in and out of the water and displaying their long wings. They twined their necks together and got closer and closer to each other. The dance finished with their beaks touching and their long curving necks making a beautiful heart shape.

Afterwards, there was a lot of wing flapping and splashing about in the water to celebrate. Tired but happy, Sofia and Dirk got out of the water and began to preen themselves with their beaks—that means they thoroughly cleaned their feathers and oiled them with the oil from a preening gland near their tails. Water birds do this because the oil waterproofs them so they can stay afloat all the time. It also keeps them warm when the water and the weather are cold.

Now there would only be a few weeks to wait before Sofia would lay her first eggs, so they would need a proper nest. Sofia and Dirk had never made a nest before of course, but wild animals have very strong instincts and they already knew how to go about it—more-or-less, that is. As they got older and more experienced, they would get better at nesting.

It was Dirk's job to pick the spot. He chose one on a strip of ground at the base of a ruined brick tower, close to the edge of the moat around to the west from the bridge. It was up on a little mound so it wouldn't be flooded if the water level rose, and the thick tower wall gave some protection from shells aimed at the town. Dirk set to work collecting material and putting it in place, pulling out reeds from the water's edge with his beak and collecting twigs that were lying around—a lot of those had been blasted off the trees since the Germans had started shelling the town.

Soon he had a big pile of vegetation built up and Sofia came over to see how he was going. She settled on top of the pile and wiggled around to make a dent in the middle where her eggs could go when the time came.

'What do you think, dear?' asked Dirk anxiously—it was up to Sofia to decide whether the location was suitable or not, and if she didn't like it Dirk would have to start again!

'I suppose it's all right for a first try. Perhaps it could be better but it will do, thank you.' (Sofia really thought the nest was very good, but she didn't want Dirk getting too pleased with himself, as he sometimes did—but Dirk really knew what she was thinking!)

'Toss me some of those reeds and twigs, please' Sofia went on, 'and we'll do some more work on it.'

The two worked happily together to finish off their nest, adding loose feathers and various bits and pieces to make a soft spot in the middle.

It was April 1915 now, and the whizz-bangs started to hit the town a lot more often than before. Buzzing aeroplanes came over too, dropping bombs that added to the damage. Sofia and Dirk had seen a few aeroplanes before the War, but now there were a lot more of them in the sky. They were bigger, faster and noisier too.

One day Dirk was sailing about, keeping an eye on the nest site, when he picked up a faint sound coming from far away to the north of the city. He could not quite make out what it was, but it made him feel very uncomfortable.

'There's something happening,' he called to Sofia, who was looking for food on the bank (she had to eat a lot before the eggs came) 'I'm going to take a look.'
'Yes, I can hear it too,' she answered. 'Be careful!'

Dirk skated along the water, flapping his wings strongly, built up speed, and rose into the air. He flew around the west side of the city, instinctively keeping away from where the whizz-bangs might be flying. Up there, he could look down on the wrecked buildings inside the walls. Then he flew north for a while, and soon realised that the sound he had heard was many humans calling out in fear. Below he saw soldiers running, some of them falling and lying still. Behind them, rolling low across the ground was a strange cloud of greenish mist.

Dirk had no idea what it was, but he knew it was something terrible—it was the cloud that the soldiers were running away from. A few small birds flew out of the cloud, then dropped to the ground like stones. A cow lumbered along and fell in a heap. Fortunately the cloud was starting to thin out in the wind. Dirk had seen enough, and he turned and flew for home, shaken by the things he had seen.

Sofia was waiting on the bank and he dropped down and settled alongside her.

'There was a green cloud. It was something very dangerous, from what I could see.' He paused for breath, then went on,

'But it was breaking up, and I don't think it will reach this far. We should be all right for now.'

Sofia, shocked and frightened, took a while to answer. She had something else on her mind too:

'I hope you're right, because this is not a good time to be leaving. I can feel my eggs are growing.'

What Dirk had seen was the first attack with poison gas, the German army's first move in what was called the Second Battle of Ypres. The gas worked at first, killing or driving away many of the French soldiers in the area. The Germans took over a lot of the territory, but a force of Canadian soldiers now came forward and stopped the Germans before they could reach the city. At first, the only way the Canadians could protect themselves from the gas was to tie wet cloths over their faces. Within a few weeks the British and French began to make proper gas masks. These were rushed to the soldiers, and later the British started to use gas themselves against the Germans. The battle finished with the German army a lot closer to Ypres but unable to get any further, so they kept blasting the city with more and more artillery shells from their big guns.

The Germans were now on the hills overlooking the city, so they could see where their shells were hitting. They could also see the roads around the city and the wagons and trucks bringing in supplies for the soldiers. Soon the wagons and the soldiers only moved at night when the darkness hid them from the German observers. Day and night, the shells exploded in the city, smashing buildings and forcing everyone below ground again for a bit of safety. Before long, it was decided that all the townspeople would have to leave. With their city being turned into a heap of rubble and the water supply and sewerage system wrecked, Ypres was not a healthy place to be. Soon there was a stream of people, mostly children, women and older men (most of the young men were in the Army) leaving the city, with their dogs and horses and whatever belongings they could carry.

Bep and Stefan went with their parents to a town called Poperinghe, ten kilometres to the west, along with many other Ypres refugees. The family had some relatives there, and they helped to build a hut for shelter, where Papa could make a living repairing shoes and boots. They were now very poor and uncomfortable, but at least they were fairly safe, out of range of the German artillery—most of the time at least.

'I wonder how our swans are getting on back there,' said Bep one day.

'They probably went away for the winter and didn't come back,' replied Mama.

'Oh yes they did come back,' put in Stefan. 'I went down to the Lille Gate a few weeks before we left, and I saw them on the water, just like before.'

'Well, you shouldn't have been out in the open like that, you could have been killed!' said Mama angrily.

The citizens were now away from the dangers of the fighting, but the soldiers stayed at ruined Ypres.

So did Sofia and Dirk. They had seen the townspeople go, but as Sofia had said, with the nest built and eggs on the way, it was no time for the swans to be leaving.

'Besides,' said Dirk, 'not all of the people have left. A lot of the other ones are still here' (by 'the other ones' Dirk meant the soldiers, their uniforms making them look different from the citizens).

One day about this time they had a reminder of just how dangerous it was around Ypres, as they watched a patrol of soldiers coming back to the city. Noticing the swans looking on in the distance, the soldiers gave them a wave. Just then a stray shell hit and exploded right where the men were. When the smoke and dust cleared, there was one stunned man getting to his feet but the others had disappeared. They had been blown to pieces by the explosion. Being wild creatures, Sofia and Dirk were pretty tough and they knew a lot about life and death. This really shocked them though; they had never seen anything so horrible before.

A few weeks after their mating dance, Sofia excitedly called to Dirk that she felt her eggs coming, as she waddled over to the nest. Sofia laid four greenish-grey eggs, one every two days. She was proud of her first laying, especially with the dangerous life experienced in their moat. After the last egg had been laid, Dirk flapped his huge wings to celebrate, and also to frighten off any other creatures that might try to steal the eggs.

Sofia covered the eggs with her body to keep them warm while the babies grew inside them (in other words, she was incubating the eggs). So began a time when Sofia would have little sleep or eat properly, because she would constantly be tending to the eggs. Every couple of hours she turned them with her beak, very careful not to cause any damage moving around in the nest. She would lose a lot of body weight and relied on Dirk to help bring her small amounts of food. She left the nest sometimes to stretch her wings, but only when Dirk was around to be on guard and take a turn keeping the eggs warm and safe.

After incubating her eggs for a few weeks, Sofia could feel some movement happening. Their first little hatchling had cracked its egg shell, and was struggling to break out. Sofia spoke encouragingly and eventually her first born tumbled out of its broken shell looking like a ball of grey fluff. Slowly two more hatchlings broke their way out into the world. Sofia continued to sit on the last remaining egg, but after a while, she realised that it wasn't going to hatch, so they had three offspring: one boy and two girl cygnets—they were going to be a family at last. The war went on around them, shells and bombs still crashing into the city, but the swans ignored them unless they came really close—they had more important things to think about now. There was nothing they could do about the war anyway, and there were babies to look after.

Parenting in Wartime

Sofia and Dirk were very proud and protective parents. At first, the cygnets nestled under Mama Sofia's body for protection, but soon the three bundles of energy wanted to explore their new surrounds, not aware of the dangers that could be all around them. Sofia, after weeks of caring for the eggs, gladly handed over some chores to Dirk. She could rest a bit, eat more and start to re-gain the weight she'd lost during incubation. All the same, the babies kept her busy. Dirk and Sofia shepherded the cygnets, trying to keep them close to the nest, helping gather food and preparing them for their first swims.

It was a funny sight to see the three little balls of fluffy grey down waddle, stumble, fall over and flutter their almost invisible stubs of wings down to the water's edge—and fall in! To their surprise, the cygnets found themselves floating, while watchful Papa Dirk kept a close eye on them. It was a lot easier for the cygnets to fall into the water than it was for them to struggle up the bank onto dry land again. This was their first lesson and it would only take them about two months to become good swimmers.

'I'm remembering the first time I tried swimming and it felt very strange being in the water,' Dirk said to Sofia, as he supervised the first swim.

'But it was exciting too,' answered Sofia.

'We need to be especially careful of the dangers in and around the moat,' Dirk warned,'but I'm going to keep us and our babies safe.'

With that he performed a great show of aggression, spreading and flapping his huge wings, stirring up the water, making quite a sight for anyone who might be around.

'You're definitely the king of the moat,' exclaimed Sofia, amused but also impressed by Dirk's exhibition.

The new hatchlings enjoyed being sheltered and protected by their parents. They loved to climb up on to their parents' backs in the water, and play hide and seek amongst the deep, soft feathers. Hitching a ride was so much fun! The three of them could easily find room on Papa's back, while trying not to slip off into the water. They constantly preened themselves, which would help them lose their grey down and get their feathers growing.

'Being a parent is tiring Dirk, but at the same time I'm very happy. I love watching the kids having fun and playing games. Let's hope the whizz-bangs stay away while they are so small,' said Sofia quietly when they were alone and their babies were hungrily feeding amongst the reeds.

'Before we know it' replied Dirk, 'they will be growing feathers and looking more like swans. So let's not think of whizz-bangs for now and enjoy our little ones.'

All the chasing around after the cygnets made Sofia quite weary, and they had been trying even Dirk's patience too. Sometimes Dirk had to be the firm disciplinarian to keep them out of harm's way. The boy cygnet, who was a bit like a junior version of Dirk, was the most adventurous. He was always wanting to paddle further and further afield, exploring.

When cygnets are about six weeks old, they start to grow proper feathers, helped by their constant preening. By the age of three to four months, their whole covering will have changed, brown feathers

taking the place of the grey down. The boy, 'junior Dirk,' was the first to start getting his feathers, and he teased his sisters with how slow they were compared to him. The girls ignored him, and went on happily chirping and cheeping to each other as they paddled around. The three youngsters were always eating, and the more they ate the bigger they grew, especially their wings. Their wingspans were getting wider all the time, and they kept flapping, building up strength for flying when they got a bit older.

At about the same time as cygnets lose their down and gain their feathers, their parents start moulting, shedding their old feathers and growing a whole new set. It is a dangerous time, because while moulting, a swan cannot fly, but thankfully, nature has arranged things so that the parents take turns. Only one parent moults at a time, so that while one parent is temporarily grounded, the other guards the family and tends to the young. The pen goes first, then the cob, so when the cygnets were a bit older, Sofia started her moulting. This took her a few weeks, then when she finished and had her beautiful new coat of pure white, Dirk took his turn.

By then the cygnets were about five months old and their wings were fully grown. With Dirk grounded while he moulted, flying instructor Sofia gathered the cygnets together,

'Well, I'm now going to give you your first flying lesson. Watch, and listen closely to what I say,' and they all took notice of their wise Mama. The first lessons were a bit of a hit and miss, with belly flops and nose dives, but it was only a week or so before all three cygnets had learnt to use their webbed feet to run over the water, flap their wings, and with speed, gain momentum to lift off into the sky and fly for the first time.

'What a proud moment for us!' exclaimed Dirk, unhappy he was sitting on the sidelines 'although I was a little anxious about the girls. After 'Junior' took off almost without a hitch, I thought they would never lift off, but they did, so I am a very happy Papa.'

'We'll see how they come down now,' Sofia said, watching them circling above.

After the three flying novices returned relatively smoothly, they swam back to their parents with chests puffed out and chirping excitedly.

'See, there was nothing to worry about,' Sofia whispered to Dirk.

'I realise that now, and well done for being their flying instructor' he replied. 'They will become more

independent now they can fly, but there are still many dangers that they are not aware of.'

Their wings were now strong enough to become airborne, and their swan-skills were getting better. They learnt to harness the wind and use their wings like a yacht uses sails. Without the need to paddle their webbed feet they could glide effortlessly over the water. The three of them had a lot of fun trying to outdo each other. They were also growing larger, and gradually changing colour from brown to eventually the beautiful white of adulthood.

One night towards the end of the year, Sofia said to Dirk,

'Well, the kids aren't kids any more. They can fly, they know how to look after themselves, and their feathers have mostly turned white. You have a job to do now.'

'I don't know what you mean,' Dirk replied.

'Yes you do. I think you should do it tomorrow morning and get it over with. Remember, I'm not happy about it either.'

What Sofia meant was that the youngsters, now over six months old, had grown into adolescent swans and it was time for them to leave their birthplace and find their own homes somewhere else, just as Sofia and Dirk and every other swan had done before. It was mainly up to the cob to make sure the young ones left. Kind-hearted Dirk was not looking forward to telling them that they must go. It was going to be unpleasant, but he knew it had to be done.

Dirk didn't sleep much that night, and it wasn't the shells and bombs that kept him awake. The next morning, he took a deep breath and paddled over to where the youngsters were getting some breakfast.

'I have something important to say,' Dirk began.

'You are all old enough to make your own lives now,' he went on, 'so it's time for you to go and find new homes. Today. Now. I think you should head in that direction to start with,' (he indicated the south-west) 'away from the whizz-bangs. Off you go now, and good luck. Mama and I will miss you, but we are swans and this is how things have to be.'

'Junior' was not really bothered.

'Don't worry, Papa,' he said, 'I was probably going to leave in the next few days anyway. I want to try something new—and maybe somewhere a bit quieter,' he added, as a big shell went off somewhere in the city. 'Thank you both for bringing us up, and good luck to you too.'

With that, he splashed along the moat, beating his wings, and rose into the air. Soon he was out of sight.

The girls were not quite as happy to go, and in the end Dirk had to scare them, hissing angrily and thrashing his wings on the water. One of them turned to her Papa, said goodbye, and asked shyly:

'Why do you and Mama really want to stay in a dangerous place like this?' and flew off for good, without waiting for the answer.

Sofia glided over to Dirk, and rubbed her long neck on his.

'It's all right,' she said gently, 'you did what you had to do. It will be easier next time. Now I know how my parents and yours must have felt when they made us go.'

'Yes, and of course if they hadn't done that we would never have met,' replied Dirk. 'It was a good question though. Why **are** we staying here, do you think?'

'This is our first home—its our place, no matter what—that's why we stay,' Sofia said, firmly.

'I think so too, and anyway, if another swan tried to take over our place, I'd fight him to the death. I'm not going to let a few whizz-bangs drive us away!' exclaimed Dirk defiantly, drawing his neck back between his wings in fighting position.

It was getting on for winter by now. Once more they would have to go away for a while to see out the really

cold time, but they would be back as soon as they could. Winter came with pouring rain at first, which didn't bother the swans especially, since they were used to being wet. For the soldiers though, it was a particularly miserable time, living in deep mud and fighting their enemies as well. Eventually the water started to freeze, so Sofia and Dirk flew west again, and found another place where it would be easier to get some food in winter. After two or three months, they felt the weather getting a little less cold. It was time to go back home again.

Making Friends

This time they were not surprised at seeing the wreckage of the city as they glided down to the water. Their spot still looked mostly unharmed, although there were now a few shell-holes nearby and some places in the wall where the bricks had been damaged. The shelling was still going on, but over a few days it seemed to Dirk that it was not as frequent as before, and there were more periods of quiet. Sofia thought the same, but a few times bursts of shells hit around the Lille Gate bridge, some of them falling into the moat with a whoosh and a roar, and throwing up great spouts of water.

This was the year 1916. Now that the buildings of Ypres had mostly been demolished, the German guns were shooting at particular targets, the roads going through the city, the railway on the western side and the two main bridges over the moat. They were trying to catch the wagons bringing supplies and the British soldiers moving in the open, mostly at night, going out to the firing line or coming back from it. To cross the moat, the soldiers had built some narrow wooden foot-bridges, hoping that the Germans would not take as much notice of them.

The temporary bridges led to small openings in the wall, called 'sally-ports', which led into the city. There was one just around from Sofia and Dirk's spot, and another one further along the moat, about half-way to the Menin Gate, where nowadays there is a modern bridge called the Poternepad Bridge.

Sofia and Dirk had only been back at Ypres for a few days when the British soldiers made an attack on a German position south of the city. Early one morning when it was still dark, the British guns near the swans' spot opened up with a deafening roar and went on shooting as fast as they could for more than an hour. Sofia and Dirk, jolted awake, put their heads under their wings and tried to keep out the noise, but that didn't really work. Finally the guns stopped firing and the swans lifted their heads, which were still ringing from the noise. That sort of thing would become a normal part of their lives now.

There were still some cold days, and snow once or twice, but things soon warmed up and the sun came out, and then it was time for Sofia and Dirk to do their mating dance again. Last year's nest had worn away by then, so Dirk gathered another pile of vegetation close to the same spot under the old tower. Since he now had some experience at nesting, the new one was better than the first. Sofia was very pleased and soon had the pile sorted into a fine nest. While Sofia and Dirk were waiting for the eggs to come, they found an unexpected source of food.

Sofia, always hungry when expecting eggs, was eating plants on the small bank near the sally-port when a British soldier came out from the city, carrying something in his hands. He listened for a while in case there were any shells coming, but all was quiet so he moved out a bit further towards where Sofia was. She stood still and waited, a bit warily, but the man stopped and tossed what he was carrying onto the edge of the water, then backed away and squatted down to watch. Sofia was very curious and after a while she paddled over to see what he had been carrying. It turned out to be food—a few pieces of torn-up bread and some cooked cabbage. She didn't hesitate long before eating it all up. It was delicious!

Dirk had wandered over now, and he was a bit disappointed to miss out. The soldier grinned and went back through the opening into the town. A few minutes later he came out again, carrying some vegetable scraps, and this time he squatted down and held out his hand holding the food. He heard the swans making little clucking and grunting noises and wondered if they could be talking to one another ...

'Can we trust him, I wonder? He's a big man, not like our little human friends from before,' said Dirk.

'I think he's just trying to be friendly,' said Sofia, 'and the food was very good!'

So they cautiously went up to the soldier, stretched their necks out to reach the food in his hand and gobbled it all (the man had also been a bit nervous—he had heard that swans can give a very nasty peck!). The swans gave him their thank-you grunts. Soldier and swans were all happy, but just then the birds heard the sound, faint at first, of an approaching whizz-bang, and scuttled as fast as they could around the corner of the wall. A few seconds later the soldier heard it too, and dashed back through the sally-port to safety, just before the shell crashed into the rampart above. He was wearing one of the new steel helmets, but that wouldn't have helped much if the shell had been closer.

Shortly afterwards, it was time for Sofia to lay eggs again. This time only two fluffy cygnets hatched out, but Sofia and Dirk were quite content to have a smaller family this season. Once again they enjoyed looking after the babies as they learnt to swim and find food, and started to grow up.

Soon they would be learning to fly. Although there were not so many whizz-bangs hitting the town now, and a lot of those came at night, it was still very important to teach the babies to quickly head for somewhere to hide when they heard one coming. That was easy when the babies were small enough to perch on their parents' backs, but they soon grew too big for that and had to swim for themselves. If Sofia or Dirk heard whizz-bangs coming, one of them would lead the way to cover, followed by the two young ones paddling as fast as they could, then the other parent bringing up the rear.

That summer, two very big battles took place to the south, in France, where the Germans fought against the French at Verdun and the British at the Somme River. Those battles lasted for months, and many thousands of soldiers lost their lives. Around Ypres, the Canadians fought a battle against the Germans near the city, at a place called Mount Sorrel, but there was a lot less fighting than before—the armies had sent many of their men and guns to France for the big battles. One fairly quiet day the general in charge of the British Army in the area of Ypres made a visit to the town to the see the situation for himself.

He was a gentle-looking old fellow with a big white moustache, and seemed rather harmless—but he was actually a very clever man and a good general. He came with a group of younger soldiers who were the officers of his staff. They first had a look over the ruined city, then went out through a sally-port

to see the moat. The general was amazed when he saw the swan family peacefully swimming about as if they didn't have a care in the world.

'Good heavens!' he said. 'Do they live here? The shelling should have scared them off long ago!'

'I've been told, sir,' replied one of the officers, 'that the cob and the pen have been here all through the war, and this is the second family they've raised.'

'Well, good luck to them,' said the general, 'I hope they make it through.'

'They don't just have to worry about the Germans, sir,' put in another officer. 'Our men sometimes shoot fish in the moat to eat, and it's only a matter of time before someone decides that roast swan would make a fine dinner!'

The general was not pleased.'We'll see about that,' he said. 'Captain, write out an order for me to sign. No soldier in my army is to harm those swans in any way, and anyone who tries to will be punished! See that the order goes out straight away.'

The general need not have worried. By now the soldiers in and around Ypres had come to look on the swans as mascots for good luck. To soldiers coming wearily back to the city from weeks fighting in the mud, the sight of the beautiful birds floating in the moat lifted their spirits.

Many of the soldiers gained fresh courage—'if a couple of swans can put up with the shelling, then so can I,' they thought. The soldiers had also worked out that if the swans suddenly disappeared into the distance, it meant that a bombardment was about to start, and they knew to take cover in a hurry.

One day that summer, a Canadian soldier, a good artist, was on the far side of the moat near the little wooden bridge, making a sketch of the ramparts. Dirk and Sofia with the two youngsters came gliding along, and he wondered if he should include them in his picture. Just then, the swans suddenly turned and began swimming fast for the bushes at the foot of the rampart wall, leaving wide wakes in the water behind them.

Moments later the soldier heard the whistle of approaching shells and threw himself flat on the ground. There were deafening crashes all around as the shells exploded, but they eventually stopped and he raised his head cautiously, very relieved to find that he was unhurt. Across the moat he could just see the white feathers of the adult swans moving among the leaves, so he knew they were all right too. The soldier finished his sketch, and now it showed the swan family swimming for safety.

In the bushes on the bank, the swans were sorting themselves out as well.

'That was a bit too close!' said Sofia. 'We've been getting rather careless lately, since it's been fairly quiet. Kids, remember when you hear that whizzing noise, head for the wall as quickly as you can!'

As well as Canadians, soldiers from all parts of the British Empire were sent to the Ypres area at different times. Towards the end of the year, some Australians arrived and noticed the swans in the moat. The feathers of one youngster were nearly all white by then, but the other still had most of her dark brown feathers. At a distance she looked almost black, and the Australians thought they were seeing a black swan like those in their own country. When they looked again a week or so later she had turned mostly white. The Australians, not knowing how young white swans changed colour, wondered where the black one had gone. Not long after that, both of the young swans had left anyway, sent away by Dirk in the same way as the first children. He found it a bit easier to do than last year, but it was still an unpleasant experience.

Soon afterwards, the signs of winter began to appear, with heavy rain and cold winds. It was not going to be the usual winter though.

'I don't remember the weather ever being this cold before,' said Dirk, 'not this early in the season anyway.'

'Yes, I think this freeze-time will be a bad one,' replied Sofia. 'We might have to go further away to find something to eat this time.'

She was right—the coming winter would be one of the coldest ever. When Sofia and Dirk took to the air, they had to fly almost to the sea-coast, fifty kilometres away, before they found a spot where there were a few scrubby plants and some grass to eat. The weather got colder and wetter as winter went on, and the swans had a miserable time, but at least they were better off than the soldiers. Inland at Ypres, it was even colder and the soldiers were stuck out in their trenches in the ice and snow, still being shot at by the enemy.

Battlefields

It was quite late into the new year (1917 to the humans) when Sofia and Dirk decided it was time to go home to Ypres again. The weather wasn't that much warmer, even though it was the start of spring, and there were still a few snow-falls. They found there were a few more pieces knocked out of the walls, and the artillery guns of both sides were still blasting away, but once more their spot was still much the same. Something else had changed, though. Sofia and Dirk did their mating dance again, but this time Sofia had a strange feeling that there would be no eggs this season. Something had upset her system—perhaps it was the cold, or the shocks of the explosions over the previous year, or both. After a while, she was sure about it.

'Dirk dear,' she said, 'you don't need to bother with a nest this year. I'm afraid there won't be a new family coming along.'

She was worried about how Dirk would take the bad news, but he was his usual easy-going self.

'Oh,' he replied, 'that's a shame, but there's always next year. This is a bit late to be having babies anyway—they wouldn't be grown up by next freeze-time. We can have a year off from being parents and just relax. Apart from the whizz-bangs of course,' he added, as another shell crashed into the town. Sofia did not answer, just swam closer and twined her neck around his.

One day a few weeks later, the German artillery guns were once more firing off hundreds of shells at the city, aiming at the area near the Lille Gate bridge. Sofia and Dirk took cover around a corner of the ramparts, where they had been safe before, bothered only by the deafening noise. This time it was different—one of the shells went astray and crashed into the rampart right above their heads. A big piece of brick flew off the wall and hit Dirk on the end of his left wing. He cried out in pain and jumped off the ground.

'What is it? What happened?' called Sofia frantically.

'My wing!' he gasped. 'Something hit me! It hurts!'

Sofia could hardly hear him amid the noise of the explosions, but she could see that his wing-tip was damaged and out of shape. She moved over and tried to comfort him while the shelling went on. Eventually it stopped and both of them calmed down a little. The pain slowly faded to a strong throbbing. The hurtling brick had broken the finger-bone at the end of his wing that supported the feathers there. Dirk twisted his head around and tried to straighten out his wing with his beak, but the pain came back and he had to stop. He had only managed to push the broken bone part of the way back into line, and there it stayed. Dirk was very careful about moving his wing over the next three or four weeks, and the bone slowly grew together again. There was not much Sofia could do to help, but she encouraged him, brought him extra food that he couldn't reach for now, and helped him with preening.

Eventually the bone healed up and stopped hurting, but the wing would never be the same again. Dirk's wing-tip stuck out at an odd angle and unbalanced him when he tried to fly—he could flap into the air but he couldn't stay there. This wasn't as much of a problem for a swan as it would have been for most other birds; swans don't do a lot of flying anyway once they have found their place to live. When winter came, though, he would not be able to fly to their usual warmer spot.

'We'll worry about that when the time comes,' said Sofia. 'For now, the weather is warming up at last, so let's enjoy it. And the wing hasn't harmed your good looks, you know!'

She was right—Dirk was fully grown by now, very big and handsome, even for a Mute Swan. He made an impressive sight as he glided on the water beside the smaller, but just as beautiful, Sofia.

Meanwhile the war went on. The Germans were still on the hills to the south and east of Ypres, from where they could look down on the city and aim their gunfire at it. The old British general with the white moustache had a long-term plan for a battle that would smash the German army on the hills, and his men had been working hard for over a year. They had secretly dug many tunnels from their own positions to places under the hills where the German trenches were, near a village called Messines. Then they packed the far ends of the tunnels with explosives. The battle started early one morning in June.

It was still dark and Sofia and Dirk were asleep on the bank near the water's edge. Many British guns a little way to the south-west had been firing away day and night for a week, but they stopped before dawn. There was a thunderstorm during the night, but that had blown over. All was quiet when suddenly the ground rocked and the water rippled. The swans jerked awake and saw a great red light appear on the low hills to the south. For a moment they thought it was the sunrise—but it was in the wrong direction to be the sun.

The great flame rippled along the hills, lighting up the clouds above and the ground below. Then, as the flames died down, a thundering roar came rolling over the city. Moments later, the guns started firing again, lighting up the horizon and adding their bursting shells to the destruction on the southern hills. For a while the swans were too amazed to move or speak, and they hardly noticed the sun coming up. Finally Sofia said,

'I hope that sort of thing won't happen too often.' For once Dirk couldn't think of anything to say.

The British soldiers had exploded their great mines under the German trenches, blowing earth

and men sky-high. After that, the German soldiers who survived were not in any condition to resist the British, who easily won the Battle of Messines. The British now held the hills south of Ypres, and turned their attention to the north-east hills. Soldiers from all parts of the British Empire, as it was called then, were in and around Ypres, getting ready for the big battles still to come—English, Scottish, Irish, Welsh, Australians, New Zealanders, and later in the year the Canadians returned also.

Things went quiet for a few weeks, then the British Army attacked the Germans again, to the north of Ypres. This time, the fighting was much harder and mostly not successful for the British. It would have taken far too long to dig another lot of tunnels, and heavy rain turned the ground to mud and made movement almost impossible. The British had to think again. They waited until the weather fined up and the ground dried out, and put the old general with the white moustache in charge once more (his name was Herbert Plumer). In September the British, Australians and New Zealanders fought several more battles against the Germans, driving them well away from Ypres. The situation was looking a lot better—for now.

For Sofia and Dirk, it was a lazy time, with no cygnets to fuss over this year. The German guns were further away, so there were not many whizz-bangs these days, and less danger. The Germans now only fired at the city sometimes, at long range. After taking turns moulting again, they both had beautiful new suits of feathers. On fine days they enjoyed sailing out on the moat and floating in the sun while they preened themselves. Often they swam around to the Menin Gate, where they saw groups of soldiers marching through the gap in the ramparts, across the bridge, and off into the distance towards the fighting. The sound of the guns was coming from some distance away now, usually just a constant rumble in the east instead of the loud crashes and bangs of before. There were even some flowers coming out,

with a few bright red patches of poppies growing in the shell-holes.

Then October came, and the weather changed again, with heavy rain most days. The swans noticed that the soldiers coming back to the city from the front line were covered in mud from head to foot.

'I wonder what's going on out there,' said Dirk one day. 'Too bad I can't fly properly any more, or I'd take a look.'

'I can go,' replied Sofia. 'I'm rather curious myself. Perhaps everything is peaceful now.'

'Or perhaps not, so be careful!' warned Dirk.

Sofia waited for a patch of clear weather, then took to the air. She flew east for a while, and all she could see below her was a filthy sea of mud, pitted by shell-holes full of dirty water. A bit further and she saw the remains of wrecked farmhouses, a few bare stumps of trees, rusty barbed wire, discarded rifles and many dead soldiers lying in the mud. Ahead Sofia could see the flashes of explosions and hear the rattle of rifles firing. She had seen enough. Horrified, she turned back and flew home to Ypres.

'It was terrible,' she told Dirk, who had been paddling up and down nervously while he waited for her. 'Nothing but mud, mess and broken things, and there were dead humans everywhere. It's much worse even than here.'

'I can see that you're really shaken up,' said Dirk. 'Now I wish I hadn't let you go. But at least we found out what's happening, and we know that we're better off here at home.'

What Sofia had seen was the battlefield near a place called Passchendaele, where one of the worst battles of the war was being fought. The rain had turned the whole area into a huge swamp and the British Empire soldiers had to struggle through the mud to move forward. All the time they were easy targets for the German soldiers shooting at them. The rain kept falling and the mud got even worse, but the surviving soldiers kept trying. At last, Canadian soldiers reached the final ridge and the ruined village that they had been aiming for. The exhausted armies settled in to get through the winter.

The Guns are Silent

Winter brought a new problem for Sofia and Dirk. With his damaged wing, Dirk could not fly to a less cold area as he had before. He would have to stay near Ypres when everything froze, and hope to find enough food to stay alive until the weather warmed up again. But what about Sofia? Dirk had a suggestion that he didn't really like making, but he thought it was for the best:

'Why don't you just go by yourself, dear?' he said. 'You can find a good spot, and I'll be all right here until you come back.'

'Don't be silly!' was her reply. 'We belong together and I'm not going anywhere without you. If you have to stay in the cold, then so do I.'

Now it was Dirk's turn to twine his neck around hers.

Somehow they got through the winter and into the new year of 1918. They ate as much as they could before the water froze over and snow fell, then scratched around for any straggly plants near the walls and under rocks. Sometimes a soldier would come out and give them some bread or leftover vegetables, which they were very grateful for. The bread wasn't really very nutritious (if the swans had been younger and still growing, it would actually have been bad for them), but it tasted good and meant they didn't feel so hungry.

Towards the end of winter they were getting better at finding food in all sorts of odd places. Then one day the ice began to melt and the plants started to grow again. The swans felt rather weak and had lost a lot of weight but they had made it through freeze-time. With enough to eat again, the swans began to put on weight and lost the bedraggled look of winter. For a while, it seemed that things might be fairly peaceful in future. Sofia started to think that if it stayed quiet, she might feel like having some babies this season. It was not to be, however.

The war was not over yet. Early in the spring, the German armies made their biggest attack yet, first in France and then in Belgium. One army attacked near Ypres and took back in a few days all the territory that had cost so many British Empire lives in the previous year. This time the Germans got closer to Ypres than ever before, apart from the few soldiers who had come and gone in 1914. Once more the city and the fields around were pounded by the big guns. But the British Army refused to give up, and finally the Germans were stopped only a few kilometres from the walls.

Both sides were exhausted, and it was months before the armies resumed serious fighting—but the British and their allies were the stronger now, and the Germans had nothing left. In the autumn, all along the battlefront from southern France to the coast of Belgium, the Allies advanced and the Germans retreated. In the north, the King of the Belgians was in charge of the armies that finally drove the Germans back to the borders of Belgium. They could go on no longer, and the war that had lasted four long years was finally over.

One morning on the Ypres moat, when it was becoming cold again, the swans were starting to think about how to get through the coming winter. For the last few weeks, they had been hearing the faint rumbling of the guns in the distance as the armies moved east. Sofia suddenly lifted her head, listened for a while, then said to Dirk,

'Listen!'

'I don't hear anything,' answered Dirk, a bit puzzled,

'That's the point,' she said. 'The whizz-bangs have stopped! Could they be gone for good this time?'

If the swans had known about clocks and calendars, they would have seen that it was eleven o'clock in the morning on the eleventh of November—the eleventh hour of the eleventh day of the eleventh month. That special time marked the end of the terrible war that had cost millions of lives.

After that, everything seemed easier in the swans' lives. With no whizz-bangs to worry about now,

Sofia decided to move house to one of the little islands in the moat. Here there were plenty of plants and grasses growing in the old shell-holes, and they had a better chance of finding food for the winter. They went rather hungry during the coldest weather, but came through it without any serious problems. At the first signs of spring in 1919, they did their mating dance again, an especially joyful one this time. Dirk picked a new spot for the nest, and soon Sofia laid a clutch of eggs. A few weeks later, they were parents again and happily raising a family of four cygnets.

Meanwhile, the townspeople began to return to their ruined city. At first there was nowhere for families to stay, with everything demolished. Bep, Stefan and their parents were still living in the little hut at Poperinghe, and one day the family decided to visit their old city to see if there was anything left. Papa borrowed a horse and cart, and soon they

were plodding up the road to Ypres. As they approached the western entrance, they were horrified by the destruction—could the city ever be the same again?

The cart passed through the Market Square, with the stump of the Cloth Hall tower still sticking up from the piles of rubble. Papa drove on down the street to find their old house.

Like the rest of the buildings, it had been smashed down to the foundations. The family gazed at the ruin sadly, then after a while Stefan said,

'Papa, we're going to walk down to the Lille Gate. We'll meet you back at the Cloth Hall later.'

Bep and Stefan were teenagers now, and their interests were changing, but they had not forgotten the swans that had fascinated them five years ago. As the two made their way along the wrecked streets, Bep said,

'You know, our swans couldn't still be here. Even if they weren't killed by the shells, they must have flown off somewhere else years ago.'

'Well, let's just see anyway.'

They climbed up the rampart alongside the Gate, picking their way over broken bricks. Stefan gazed up and down the moat, then:

'See over there!' he said, pointing at the two white patches in the water near the far bank.

They climbed down to the road again, crossed the bridge and ran along the bank. Sure enough, there were the swans, floating in the moat just as before—except that:

'Look, they have babies now! Four of them! Aren't they beautiful?' exclaimed Bep, feeling her eyes filling with tears.

'Still here, after all this,' said Stefan quietly. 'How brave must they be.'

Seeing the two young people, the swans paddled up close to the bank, shepherding the cygnets along. Sofia and Dirk chirped and nodded in greeting.

'You know,' said Sofia 'I'm sure these humans are our small friends from the old times, grown much bigger. I'm very glad to see them.'

'Yes, me too' Dirk replied. 'It looks as though things really will get back to normal in the end.'

They puffed up their necks in the swan sign of happiness.

Peace and a Great Monument

While the years of rebuilding were getting under way, Sofia and Dirk found out again what a peaceful life was like. Although there was no longer any danger and excitement, there was still plenty happening to interest them. The terrible sounds of war were replaced by the happier sounds of saws, hammers and chisels as the building work went on. Gradually the roofs and spires rose again behind the ramparts. Near their place in the moat, the Lille Gate was rebuilt, the ramparts were repaired and new trees were planted. A great memorial to the soldiers was built at the Menin Gate.

A few of the other water birds returned to the moat—including some ducks, to Sofia's annoyance—but no other swans. Each year another family of cygnets was born, to be looked after and brought up, but Sofia and Dirk were getting older and the time came when there would not be any more babies.

One day in the summer of 1927, when the swans were getting towards the end of their lives, they went for a sail in the sun up the moat towards the Menin Gate. Sofia and Dirk could see a huge crowd of people gathered around the big new memorial building and along the repaired bridge and the ramparts, townspeople and visitors in their best clothes. There were also many soldiers in colourful uniforms, who had now come not to fight but to remember in a great ceremony. In the crowd were Bep with her husband and Stefan with his wife, proud and honoured to be there. As they waited for the formalities to begin, their thoughts went back to the bleak days of the war that tore up their lives and destroyed their beloved home city.

The swans had the feeling that something important was about to happen, and they stopped paddling and waited on the water nearby. Some distinguished people stood on a platform and made speeches to the crowd. One of them was old General Plumer, still with his white moustache, the same man who had led the armies at Ypres—and who had ordered his men to protect the swans. He spoke of the 'Missing' soldiers whose names were engraved on the walls:

'He is not missing. He is here.'

Finally the tall figure of King Albert rose to speak of the unbreakable links between the British Army and the Belgian people. When he had finished, the sad haunting music of a bugle came drifting over the water to where the swans floated, watching and listening. The music stopped and the whole crowd was silent for one minute, then another bugle call rang out. After a while the crowd began to move off. A small group of younger people lingered on the bridge, gazing at the two swans floating quietly on the moat. Bep and Stefan were both lost in wonder at how the swans they had delighted in seeing over the years of war and peace had survived for so long. Then they turned away, with the tingly feeling that when they each had families of their own, what an amazing story they would tell their children.

Sofia and Dirk waited on the water for a long time after the crowd moved off. They were both thinking about what had just happened and the lives they had led in the past.

'That music made me feel sad and proud at the same time,' said Sofia, 'and I'm thinking about the awful time years ago when the whizz-bangs came every day.'

'But we got through it all, and we are still together and still in our home. We raised a lot of young swans too,' replied Dirk. 'That's something we can be proud of.'

He glanced over at Sofia and thought once again how beautiful she was, just as she had been all those years ago when they first met. The sun was going down as they turned and slowly swam back towards the Lille Gate.

That ceremony was the official opening of the Menin Gate Memorial on 24 July 1927. From 1930, interrupted only for a few years by another terrible war in Europe, the people of Ypres have held a ceremony at the Menin Gate every night, every single night, where the moving bugle call 'The Last Post' is played. The call is in memory of the soldiers who died in the war defending Ypres. In spite of everything, the British and Empire armies had never abandoned the city—and neither had the Swans of Ypres.

Note from the Authors to our Readers

At the beginning of the book we wrote that 'this is the story of two particular swans, a male and a female, who lived in the Ypres moat during the most dramatic time in the city's history'. It may have seemed that the story of the swans just came from our imaginations, as a different way of presenting a piece of history, a summary of the 1914 to 1918 war in Belgium and France.

We think it may surprise you to know that this is not entirely a book of fiction, but is based on fact. There really were two very brave swans who lived through the time of terrible destruction of the city of Ypres. Of course, the 'conversations' of the swans and many of the smaller details are imagined, but on the following pages are extracts from factual books and other records that mention the swans. These were written by people who were alive at the time and most of them actually saw what they were writing about.

Let's start with a poem by Dorothy Stuart that appeared in the magazine *Punch* in 1919:

THE SWANS OF YPRES

Ypres was once a weaving town,
Where merchants jostled up and down
And merry shuttle used to ply;
On the looms the fleeces were
Brought from the mart at Winchester,
And silver flax from Burgundy.

Who is weaving there to-night?
Only the moon, whose shuttle white
Makes silver warp on dyke and pond;
Her hands fling veils of lily-woof
On riven spire and open roof
And on the haggard marsh beyond.

No happy ghosts or fairies haunt
The ancient city, huddling gaunt,
Where wagons crawl with anxious wheel
And o'er the marshland desolate
Wind slowly to the battered gate
That Flemings call the Gate of Lille.

Yet by some wonder it befalls
That, where the lonely outer walls
Brood in the silent pool below,
Among the sedges of the moat
Like lilies furled, the two swans float;
'The Swans of Ypres' men call them now.

They have heard guns and many men
Come and depart and come again.
They have seen strange disastrous things,
When fire and fume rolled o'er their nest;
But changeless and aloof they rest,
The Swans of Ypres, with folded wings.

This is from a book called *Warrior*, written in 1932 by an officer of the British Army, Graham Hutchison; from page 192:

> *... although Nature in her woods and orchards, crops and grass-lands perished under high explosive and gas attacks, in the moat which lay to the east of the ancient buttressed ramparts of Ypres, two swans, male and female, could daily be observed making their stately swim around the moat, like a general and his aide-de-camp inspecting billets in a back area. And each year, in the spring, the swans built their nest and brought up their family. The children winged away to safer habitations, while the parents remained as the mascots and guardians for the successive Divisional Headquarters which were dug into the ramparts behind.*

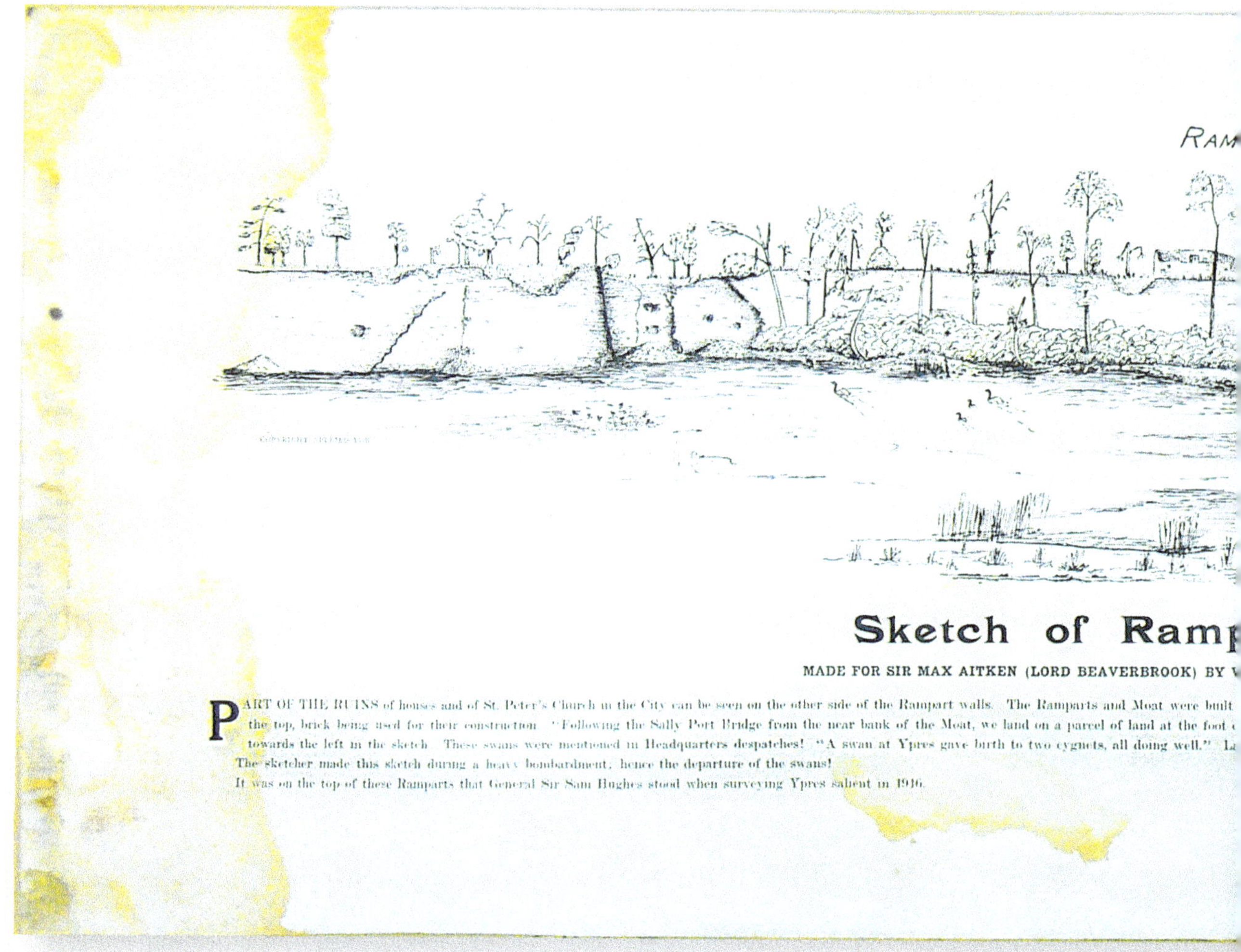

Here is the sketch drawn by the Canadian soldier that we mentioned on Page 38. His name was Walter Draycott, and he did the drawing in June of 1916:

Looking closely at the left-centre of the picture, you can see the swan family swimming quickly towards the wall.

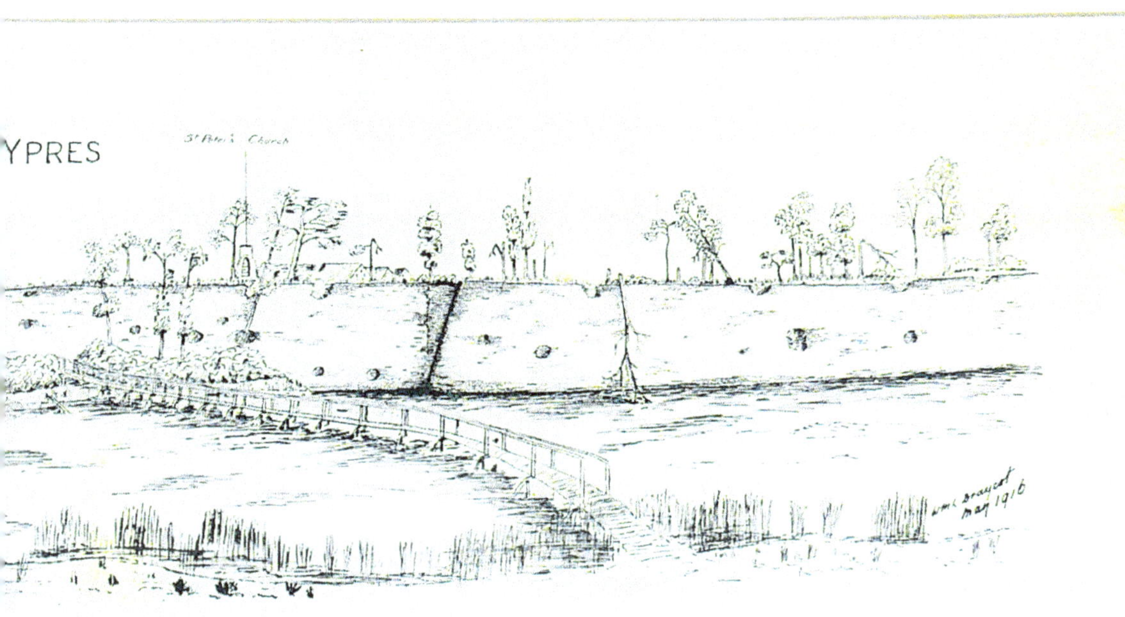

Moat at Ypres

PATRICIAS," ATTACHED TO INTELLIGENCE DEPARTMENT

ithstood many an assault. It will be noticed that they are pitted and broken by shells of large calibre. They stand about 20 to 25 feet in height, being 15 feet thick at o the left, enter the Sally Port and proceed through a long tunnel which brings us within the City." Two swans with their two cygnets are seen on the Moat going n the top of the Rampart walls, but many have fallen victims to German shellfire.

W. M. L. DRAYCOT.
Princess Pats, Intelligence Department.

Walter wrote within the picture's caption:

> *These swans were mentioned in Headquarters despatches! 'A swan at Ypres gave birth to two cygnets, all doing well' ... The sketcher made this sketch under a heavy bombardment, hence the departure of the swans!*

On the 13th of September 1917, an Australian officer made this entry in an official Army document, the War Diary of the 10th Australian Field Artillery Brigade, which at the time had its headquarters office within the Ypres ramparts:

> *Two large white swans live in the moat on the east side of Ypres. Both are very tame and feed from the hand—it is reported that they have been here since the war began. One was hit in the wing with a shrapnel pellet but has recovered.*

Here are two extracts from *The War the Infantry Knew,* by J C Dunn (page 392, 393 and 412):

> *September 25th [1917]: ... Ypres is a ghost: the little town will have to be rebuilt, every house, from its foundations. The ramparts are scarred, but stand. Only the moat is unchanged. On its calm surface there floated, so still as to make scarcely a ripple, two swans preening themselves languidly in the brilliant, oppressive sun of a fine day.*
>
> *October 24th [1917]: Clear and sharp. The swans from the Lille Gate sailed around this morning. The cob, a great beauty, appears to have been wounded; one of the digits of his left wing looks as if it had been broken and had set badly. These birds have become legendary. Their appearance at the Menin Gate foretells a peaceful day, their disappearance, no one knows whither, portends a bombardment.*

This is a part of a newspaper article that appeared in the *Yorkshire Evening Post* on the 22nd of May, 1918:

> *Of all the strange things which those of us who know the terrible Ypres salient have ever seen there, perhaps the most surprising is the small family of swans which live in the moat below the ramparts of the stricken city ... These ramparts have not only withstood the wear and tear of ages, but also the solid brick walls have turned an unbroken face to the fiercest artillery which ever assailed a city. Pitted and scarred they may be, but they will never be moved, and underneath the protection of the heavy walls live the swans of Ypres.*
>
> *The birds have lived in the shrapnel-swept moat since the beginning of the war, surviving the terrible bombardments of three long years. They are still to be seen gliding peacefully on the water as if they disdained the little war of the nations of men.*

All soldiers know the swans of Ypres, and when they started to build their nest last season many were the bets as to the probable length of their stay there.

On one occasion a German shell fell within a short distance of the nest, but the brave sitting bird, except that she fluttered a moment from the concussion, took no notice of the devastation.

... The swans still remain in the old moat, and the spring of 1918 sees them, perhaps a trifle less agile.... It may be they are on rations, self-imposed. But at any rate, they will never surrender their moat to all the force that Krupp can fling against the battered area and town of Ypres.

(Krupp was a German manufacturer of weapons)

This is a New Zealand item, from the book *Official History of the New Zealand Engineers During the Great War, 1914—1918,* by L.M. Shera (page 173):

The Ypres Moat is still inhabited by a pair of beautiful white swans, which had survived all the piled misfortunes of this unhappy city. Their safety and rights as original inhabitants were guarded by an Army order, and they were still there late in 1918, and may even yet be paddling around lamenting the absence of the stir of bygone days.

That was published in 1927, the year that the Menin Gate Memorial was opened. General Plumer's friend and chief assistant, General Charles Harington, wrote a book about him, *Plumer of Messines.* On pages 301 and 302, about Plumer's great speech at the opening ceremony, Harington wrote, first remembering Ypres during the war:

The Cloth Hall of world fame. The Cathedral. The Convent. The old Water Tower leaning over like Pisa, and every other building, all in ruins, the old swans still swimming in the moat ...

and then the speech:

... His rendering of 'He is not missing; he is here' will long be remembered as a comfort and inspiration to the parents and others who heard it. All was hushed. Even the swans which I had watched swimming about in the moat seemed to understand. They or their parents had been shelled day and night for nearly four years.

Here are two photographs, both from the Australian War Memorial's collection; the first one we think is from 1916, although the date is given as '?1917'. Two young swans are in the centre of the picture, one still with its darker feathers. The second photo is dated as October 1917. Both were probably taken with the photographer standing on the Lille Gate bridge. You can see how the ramparts were battered by the artillery shells. At the right of each picture, the ramparts make a right-angled bend; the moat continues around from there and leads up to the Menin Gate.

Australian War Memorial P00437.020

Australian War Memorial C00446

This beautiful scene, painted by Jozef Quisthoudt in1948, shows a pair of swans gliding along the moat near the Lille Gate—'Sofia' and 'Dirk' must have looked like this on the many times they travelled up to the Menin Gate during the Great War. Other swans like those pictured here lived in the Ypres moat before and after the War, but there have been no long-term residents in recent times.

We hope you enjoyed reading this book as much as we enjoyed writing it. The further we researched material, and discovered more information, it seemed that the swans, 'Sofia' and 'Dirk', came to life. We developed a firm affection for those two brave swans who lived in the moat of Ypres throughout the First World War, in almost constant danger, yet continued with their natural lives. They have waited over a century for their story to be told, and it is our honour to bring it to light.

Bibliography

Books and Magazines:

Beckett, I.F.W. *Ypres: The First Battle 1914.* London, 2004.

Birkhead, M and Perrins, C. *The Mute Swan.* London, 1986.

Dendooven, D. *Menin Gate and Last Post.* Koksidje, Belgium, 2001.

Dunn, J.C. *The War the Infantry Knew.* London,1994.

Harington, Sir C. *Plumer of Messines.* London,1935.

Holt, T and V. *Major and Mrs Holt's Battlefield Guide to the Ypres Salient and Passchendaele.* Barnsley, UK, 2011.

Hutchison, G.S. *Warrior.* London, 1932.

Palmer, A. *The Salient: Ypres 1914—18.* London, 2007.

Price, A.L. *Swans of the World: In Nature, History Myth & Art.* Oklahoma, USA, 1994

Nicolaides, M. *Swan Life.* UK, 2015

Punch magazine, 1919.

Schuyl, M. *The Swan: A Natural History.* Ludlow, UK, 2012

Shera, L.M. *Official History of the New Zealand Engineers during the Great War, 1914—1918.* Wanganui, NZ, 1927.

Yorkshire Evening Post. May 1918.

Websites:

www.theswansanctuary.org.uk

swanlovers.net

www.greatwar.co.uk/ypres-salient

www.walterdraycot.com

www.greatwarchronicle.ca (for Walter Draycott's diary)

Acknowledgements

We are indebted to the soldiers who recorded the historical data found during research into the Great War history of an Australian Army unit. These records became the foundation of this book.

Many thanks to Catherine Gordon for her superb paintings which have enhanced the book immeasurably.

Our special thanks also to Dominick Dendooven, Historian at the In Flanders Fields Museum, Ieper, Belgium who kindly gave us the benefit of his great knowledge and made many helpful comments on the original manuscript.

We are grateful to Valerie O'Connor and her daughters, Alena and Isla Harvey, who happily took up the offer to be our first young readers and gave us appreciated suggestions.

Thanks to the late Coral Langford; Estelle Blackburn; the late Brian Dawson; Heather Cooper; Michael Muntz; and Genelle Jones, for their enthusiastic encouragement after viewing the manuscript in its raw form.

Our gratitude also goes to Patrick Brion of the Belgian military archives, and to Max Uechtritz, producer of the documentary *The Menin Gate Lions,* for their help and encouragement.

We acknowledge the Northam Shire located in the Avon River Valley, Western Australia, for protecting and caring for a small colony of Mute swans, a rarity in Australia, the only country in the world in which black swans are natural inhabitants.

Photographs on pages 62 and 63 reproduced by permission of the Australian War Memorial Collection:

P00437.020; C00446

Jozef Quisthoudt painting *View of the Ypres fortifications and Lille Gate* (1948) on page 64 reproduced by permission of collection Yper Museum, Ieper, Belgium.

We have endeavoured to trace copyright holders for permission to reproduce material that may still be subject to copyright, but given the lapse in time since original material was produced, this has not been possible. The authors apologise for any errors or omissions and would appreciate notification of any corrections.

www.ingramcontent.com/pod-product-compliance
Lightning Source LLC
LaVergne TN
LVHW060602110826
845154LV00003B/20
9780648854593